2015 Annual
BEST IDEAS

★ ★ ★ ★ ★ ★ ★

America *inBloom*
Planting pride in our communities

Tarboro, NC

Printed in USA by Createspace
ISBN-13: 978-1517030506
ISBN-10: 1517030501

America in Bloom envisions communities across the country as welcoming and vibrant places to live, work, and play—benefiting from colorful plants and trees; enjoying clean environments; celebrating heritage; and planting pride through volunteerism.

America in Bloom is a 501(c)(3) non-profit organization.

This book was made possible by volunteers.
Concept - Leslie Pittenger
Editing - Leslie Pittenger and Evelyn Alemanni
Design, layout, print coordination - Evelyn Alemanni

America in Bloom
2130 Stella Ct. Columbus, OH 43215
614-453-0744   aib@AmericaInBloom.org
www.AmericaInBloom.org

Calabasas, CA

★ 2015 Annual Contents ★

Cover images:

Top row: Calabasas, CA; Holland, MI; Rockford, IL

Center row: Lewes, DE; Lexington, KY; Washington, MO

Bottom row: Catskill, NY; Morro Bay, CA

Photos limited to those submitted by participants and judges.

About America in Bloom

As we travel across America, some towns are more striking than others. They appear cleaner, prettier, more welcoming. We may feel comfortable in their ambiance without knowing exactly why. These are the places where we want to spend time, maybe even relocate there. Chances are these towns are some of the many America in Bloom (AIB) participants.

Our country is experiencing a resurgence of residents who want to be actively involved in their communities, addressing many urgent needs. America in Bloom is providing the framework to get the job done via its annual awards program.

Plan to participate in the America in Bloom program year after year for the boost it can give your town. Information is available at www.AmericaInBloom.org. With America in Bloom you can dig in and plant pride in your city.

America in Bloom is a 501(c)(3) nonprofit organization. Our board members and judges are all volunteers.

 ## The Best Ideas Book Series

The Best Ideas book series was conceived when Evelyn Alemanni, one of the AIB judges, realized the importance of sharing all the great ideas she was seeing while judging towns across the United States. There have been several editions, culminating in the *Ten Years of Best Ideas* published in 2012. That book offers more than 2000 best practices and photos and is arranged by evaluated criteria.

This annual update showcases the best ideas from 2015 AIB participants. It features best ideas submitted in community profiles. Some of the text has been edited for space considerations. The Special Mentions were excerpted from evaluations written by 2015 AIB judges.

If you don't yet own the *Ten Years of Best Ideas* book, you can order it at www.AmericaInBloom.org. Additional copies of this addendum can also be ordered there as well. We hope you enjoy the *Best Ideas* book and this addendum and find many useful ideas and programs for your town.

Holliston, MA

★ Arroyo Grande, California

Special Mention: Heritage Preservation

Since the days of the Chumash Indians, the area that is now Arroyo Grande has been a center for agriculture in California's Central Coast. Celebration of the agricultural heritage of the area occurs throughout the year. The Strawberry Festival draws thousands of visitors over Memorial Day weekend. Celebrating its 78th year in 2015, the Harvest Festival held in September focuses on locally grown vegetables, flowers and fruit.

Best Idea: Inasmuch as California is having its worst drought in 156 years, it has been necessary to create water saving programs at all levels. Arroyo Grande in Bloom is working to set an example by planting drought tolerant plants and converting watering systems to drip or eliminating them where possible. The city has removed 33,000 square feet of turf and changed hundreds of sprinkler heads to a more water efficient delivery style. Some areas will be converted to drought resistant plantings and other areas covered with either mulch or decomposed granite. The projected saving of potable water is 1.8 million gallons, which represents about a 50% reduction in water use in the affected areas. Visit http://ca-arroyogrande.civicplus.com/DocumentCenter/View/2060 to view details.

★ Belpre, Ohio

Special Mention: Urban Forestry

Belpre has an impressive number of large trees, some in beautifully maintained public parks. Others are protected and proudly featured in private gardens. A "Historic Grove" has 27 mature trees that lend a special character to the park. An active Tree Commission encourages tree protection, planting of new trees and champions proper pruning and mulching. Belpre values its tree canopy and is protecting and preserving its urban forest.

Best Idea: An idea that we brought back from the 2014 AIB symposium was using the design of our AIB participation plaque as a street sign announcing our accomplishments. We had signs made and placed them in 10 locations. They complement wayfinding signs and other street signs. This is just another way to let the community know what is happening and how they can make a difference!

★ Brewton, Alabama

Special Mention: Overall Impression

Brewton is comprised of some spectacular elements: wonderfully preserved, restored and repurposed buildings; state-of-the-art educational facilities; an expansive and expanding park system; lush and lovely landscaping; and myriad festivals and community events that all add up to an enviable quality of life for its residents.

Best Idea: Brewton is getting a new look. Working with graphic artists, we have developed proposals on updated logo design and better advertising strategies. Banners were designed and installed featuring iconic images from the city including blueberries, antebellum homes and azaleas, longleaf pines and kayaking on waterways. The new banners brighten streets and welcome residents and visitors. Park signage has also been redesigned.

★ Calabasas, California

Special Mention: Heritage Preservation

Calabasas has ordinances to protect existing historic and natural resources. The attention to viewshed preservation is another example of their heritage awareness. A historic adobe farmstead museum and collection of historic documents at the library bear testament to the importance Calabasas gives to its past.

Best Idea: Even before the onset of California's most severe recorded drought, Calabasas began reviewing the irrigation system in its parks and rights of way.

Phase one constituted the conversion and consolidation of 58 pre-existing controllers into 52 weather-based evapotranspiration smart controllers in all city-owned facilities, street parkways, medians, city parks and freeway interchanges. The internet-based system allows administrators to change, update, and upload watering programs at any time and notifies them by phone and/or email when any program changes are made in the field. Controllers can also send out a variety of status notifications and if a pipe bursts or sprinkler heads break, once maximum set flow rates are exceeded, automatic shutoff valves are triggered.

Phase two constitutes a major upgrade and expansion for the reclaimed water irrigation system. Calabasas is the first city in California to implement a citywide smart irrigation control system.

★ Castle Rock, Washington

Special Mention: Floral Displays

The floral display at Castle Rock's gateway is second to none. It is as colorful and well maintained as any garden in the country. Store owners are even equipped with baggies full of plant tags so that visitors or residents who want to know the varieties of flowers used will have their questions answered.

Best Idea: Our BEST IDEA for 2015 was actually initiated in 2012. The new downtown streetscape had lamp posts with banner brackets. However, there was no funding for banners, so we called on business, city, and community leaders to form the Castle Rock Street Art Committee. With assistance from CRHS shop students, MDO plywood was cut into the shape of salmon and sold to area artists, students and residents to decorate. The street art was hung from the banner brackets all summer and taken down in the fall. Some artists chose to donate their art and these were auctioned to raise more funds.

★ Catskill, New York

Special Mention: Heritage Preservation

Catskill must be seen through many lenses to appreciate its breadth of commitment to preserving its heritage. The East Side Historic District offers a tapestry of architectural styles which preserve a special slice of 19th century. The Thomas Cole National Historic Site celebrates the founder of America's first major art movement, the Hudson River School. Unspoiled natural heritage is enjoyed at the RamsHorn-Livingston Sanctuary. Catskill's respect for heritage provides for a rich today and an exciting tomorrow.

Best Idea: Our Best Idea is to continue what we are doing with Cultivate Catskill – to make it a coordination entity for the Village for any future improvements. Our goals are to establish maintenance solutions for our watering and general clean-up of streets and parks. We are still hoping to interest more individuals to be prideful in our community and to join our forces to make all this one concerted effort for improving our Village of Catskill.

★ Combined Locks, Wisconsin

Special Mention: Landscaped Areas

Very attractive signage announces various parks and recreation areas. These signs are in landscaped beds that are well maintained, colorful and welcoming, showing pride and cooperation within this community. Trails offer well-constructed bridges and perfectly maintained, weed-free paths. Homes are neatly manicured with beautiful gardens.

Best Idea: In Combined Locks, most of the summer activity revolves around ball fields which are very costly to light. Seven years ago we started the "Light those Lights" event to raise money for the continuous improvements at Memorial Park. The effort and results keep growing each year.

★ Echo, Oregon

Special Mention: Heritage Preservation

Echo has a rich heritage starting with three noteworthy Oregon Trail sites. Ten historical places and two museums depict Echo from its founding in 1880 and before. With limited resources, the stories are told of the struggles and challenges of the Native American tribes, early settlers, immigrants, and the development of the railroad in 1883. Echo is the recipient of the Oregon Heritage Excellence Award.

Best Idea: The Downtown Project remains our Best Idea in decades. The improvements blend with the Piercy's commercial improvements, particularly the Koontz building renovation. The historic ambience remains while custom improvements such as benches, street lights, planters, bike racks, etc., make it uniquely Echo in style. It is also a project that Echo residents and visitors have been excited about and our donations for America in Bloom projects have increased as a result.

★ Edmonston, Maryland

Special Mention: Landscaped Areas

Edmonston is establishing an edible forest by planting American Persimmon trees, Paw Paw trees, and Serviceberry trees near the recreation center. Residents are encouraged to harvest the fruit and use it in meals.

Best Idea: Edmonston's Best Idea for 2015 was the decision to participate in America in Bloom. The reports generated by the judges are an invaluable resource in assisting communities that participate to strive to improve the quality of life of their residents.

In order to implement Edmonston in Bloom, the town tapped into an amazing existing resource – the Edmonston Green Team. The Green Team consists of community volunteers and elected officials that focus on sustainability and environmental awareness.

The Edmonston Green Team and Edmonston in Bloom reinforce the town motto – "Green is not just our color—it's our way of life."

★ Estes Park, Colorado

Special Mention: Overall Impression

With a visionary town leadership, dedicated city employees and civic-minded volunteers work tirelessly to ensure that the residents of Estes Park are constantly reminded of the beauty of the wilderness that surrounds them. Throughout the community – in residential and commercial areas alike – there is a sense of pride of place and a willingness to work together to keep Estes Park blooming!

Best Idea: The primary reasons Estes Park is so special and popular with guests is the magnificent views of Rocky Mountain National Park that surround the village, the wildlife, and the clean mountain air. This beautiful place depends on a healthy environment and its stewardship. To assure the preservation of wide open spaces the Town of Estes Park recently contracted to purchase two parcels of land in the Kiowa Ridge subdivision. Plans are to use a portion of that land to expand the trail system in the Estes Valley.

★ Fairhope, Alabama

Special Mention: Urban Forestry

Fairhope is serious about preserving and protecting its impressive tree canopy. A tree committee provides public input into improving and preserving trees, provides definitions for heritage trees and means for their protection. There are suggestions for overstory, understory, and exotic trees, and for evergreen and bio-retention plantings.

Best Idea: Today, in a nod to the mission of our forefathers, our Mayor and City Council have the vision to take a tract of land purchased last fall and keep it as a green gateway into Fairhope. This is our Best Idea and one that is supported by the residents of Fairhope.

Approximately 3.2 miles of new passive trails will be developed on a parcel of 34 acres of undeveloped land on a critical watershed (Fly Creek). The new trails will connect with the existing Eastern Shore Trail, one of Alabama's 15 National Recreation Trails, and will provide natural resource-based outdoor recreation activities. Currently, the watershed is being transformed from woodlands, pastures and cropland into residential and commercial areas with expanded roadways. Approximately 285 acres of wetlands within the watershed provide natural food storage, groundwater replenishment, habitats for freshwater and marine species and key terrestrial animals, corridors for wildlife passages, and aesthetic green space for residents. The rapid population growth in this area of Baldwin County and the likely continuation of this pattern have created a sense of urgency for the need to restore and preserve the natural resources within the watershed. The protection and preservation of this land is not just a dream of city leaders, it is the desire of the people of Fairhope. With the city's acquisition of this 34-acre tract, the last remaining large area of undeveloped property in the lower Fly Creek area, a diversity of scarce habitats including forested wetlands and longleaf pine forests will be preserved for outdoor recreational uses for residents and visitors for years to come.

★ Fairview Park, Ohio

Special Mention: Landscaped Areas

Fairview Park has beautiful natural areas in Bain Park. Many of the neighborhoods are defined by their attractive landscapes and large trees. Commendations to the Garden Club, Green Team and other volunteers for their work to improve landscapes all over the city.

Best Idea: The Best Idea the Fairview Park community chose to implement in 2015 is the development of a community-wide civic beautification strategy. Members of Fairview Park's America in Bloom Steering Committee intend to use the judges' evaluation as a foundation for identifying areas of improvement. Our theory is that a community has difficulty viewing itself objectively due to over familiarization. We welcome the fresh perspective of our America in Bloom judges.

★ Gallipolis, Ohio

Special Mention: Heritage

Gallipolis' rich history is evident in its three cemeteries. The prohibition days monument marker in Mound Hill Cemetery holds the secrets of moonshiners. Restaurateur Bob Evans is interred nearby on the summit of the hill overlooking the river and a bench displays his signature hat. Headstones at the Pine Street Cemetery date back to the Revolutionary War. Adjacent on Pine Street, past residents from the African American community are interred. The community recognizes the value of these sites and continues to show respect to the departed through the care of these facilities.

Best Idea: This year, we co-hosted the first Miss Gallipolis in Bloom pageant with Bossard Memorial Library. Eight girls from the 4th, 5th and 6th grades entered the contest and the winner will reign and participate at all our events throughout the year. This was not a beauty contest, but chooses a child who can speak well and be informed about GIB projects so that she can tell others about AIB ideals.

★ Greendale, Indiana

Special Mention: Floral Displays

Greendale, a perfect example of a blooming community, has scores and scores of hanging baskets adorning lamp poles and street signs. Water-saving containers have reduced watering. The colorful use of petunias, sweet potato vines and angel wing begonias provide an eye-catching arrangement. There are also floral displays in front of all city offices, many businesses and residences.

Best Idea: We are proud of our 11 years of participation in the America in Bloom program. We pore over our evaluation each year and earmark recommendations we consider a good fit for our community, implementing those recommendations as resources permit. We identify the historic Greendale Cabin as the center of our small-town, big-hearted identity. We invested a great deal in updating the interior of the cabin over the winter, and are now completing exterior work.

★ Hammond, Louisiana

Special Mention: Heritage Preservation

Hammond is recognized for the care and attention to the preservation of the tangible history as well as the respect for its heritage trees. The involvement in this cultural effort includes all age groups and greatly strengthens Hammond as a special place to be.

Best Idea: The revitalization of Zemurray Park has had a tremendous effect on historic downtown Hammond and surrounding neighborhoods and schools. Turtles, ducks, and other wildlife have attracted people to the park. Some people fish the restocked pond, others canoe or kayak. A new playground has given children aged 5 to 12 a safe, fun, large space to play. There's free Wi-Fi, an outdoor fitness park, and plans for much more.

★ Henderson County, North Carolina

Special Mention: Heritage Preservation

Throughout Henderson County non-profit organizations and historic preservation commissions work to preserve the aesthetics of the region. Numerous districts and landmarks within the county have received local designation. Historic Flat Rock, Inc., a 501(c) dedicated to preserving the heritage of the area, has a very active volunteer base which raises funds to purchase at-risk historic properties.

Best Idea: The serpentine Main Street features planted areas and boxes brimming with seasonal flowers and trees, tables and chairs for relaxing, and two water features. The completion of this project is an asset to our community and our Best Idea in 2015!

★ Holland, Michigan

Special Mention: Environmental Efforts

Holland Energy Park is replacing a coal-fired generating plant with a new, more sustainable natural gas facility. The project will eradicate three species of invasive weeds and is recycling much of the demolition materials on-site. Upon completion Holland Energy Park will connect to Outdoor Discovery Center Macatawa Greenway, a 2500-acre conservation and outdoor education system connected by trails along the Macatawa River.

Best Idea: Locally-owned and operated power generation has been a key factor to Holland's vitality and economic success over the past century. To meet demand, we used an inclusive, community-driven process to identify a variety of different options. The results pointed toward construction of a combined cycle natural gas plant, supplemented by the purchase of wind energy from existing providers. This will result in dramatic reductions in greenhouse gases and particulate emissions, while achieving significant gains in energy and cost efficiency.

★ Holliston, Massachusetts

Special Mention: Community Involvement

Holliston has many volunteer commissions and boards that exercise significant influence over the community's direction. The key ingredient for the success of volunteerism in Holliston is the extensive collaboration between different groups and prevailing "can-do" attitude.

Best Idea: The AIB Best Ideas book gave us the path needed to make a significant impact on a community problem by providing ideas and techniques that would work on a walkway project connecting the municipal parking lot to Central Street and downtown. There was collaboration involving the City Selectmen, the fire department, the town administrator, businesses, Holliston in Bloom, and the garden club. Volunteers provided heavy equipment, labor, landscaping, engineering drawings, and materials. An old wall needed to be moved to make the walkway safe and usable. Concrete walls were built, plants were donated and planted, lines were painted, the highway department planted grass, and local art students are painting murals.

The new walkway is a project that brought the community together and made a difference.

★ Hopkinsville, Kentucky

Special Mention: Overall Impression

Hopkinsville has added many new improvements to complement the attractive parks and memorials throughout town. The new gateway sign welcomes drivers from the interstate highway and new wayfinding signage helps direct visitors to important sites, including the new Greenway that follows the river through town.

Best Idea: The City of Hopkinsville recently completed another segment of its beautiful Greenway System linking the downtown and public library to neighborhoods and parks. This multi-phase trail allows pedestrians, bicyclists and skaters to enjoy the outdoors in a beautiful, safe environment. Woodland overlooks, restrooms, and maps with points of interest are provided.

★ Independence, Louisiana

Special Mention: Not applicable as this town registered as "non-compete".

Best Idea: School gardens and community gardens are wonderful educational venues to teach such things as plant selection, soil preparation, and composting to both young and old. The Head Start facility in Independence features a raised children's garden in the play yard.

★ Lewes, Delaware

Special Mention: Floral Displays

The municipality, businesses and residents work hard at creating spectacular floral displays. Hanging baskets abound. Containers of all sizes, shapes and colors are artistically planted and lovingly groomed twice a week to achieve long-lasting attractive displays. It seems that the water has love in it.

Best Idea: Our Best Idea is the complete design, landscaping and planting at the Post Office in honor of its 100th Anniversary. This highlights an important aspect of our historic town and a number of community members came together to contribute their particular expertise to the project. The land around the post office was re-scaped using private donations and in-kind services. A local nursery donated the plants, a local company donated and installed the sprinkler system, and Lewes in Bloom volunteers planted the perennials and annuals and maintain the garden. It is now a focal point for residents and visitors and underscored our philosophy of using native plants where possible.

★ Lewisburg, West Virginia

Lewisburg's proud history is reflected in its buildings and the residents who maintain them. It has been recognized by the National Trust for Historic Preservation as one of the nation's Dozen Distinctive Destinations. Three historic cemeteries, the North House Museum, and handsome, architecturally significant private homes tell the rich local story. The city's cultural heritage includes one of only four Carnegie Halls in existence and two thriving farmers markets.

Best Idea: The vision of the Lewisburg Downtown Business Association (LDBA) was to create more visibility for Lewisburg in order to increase the number of visitors to this art oriented and historic destination. The positive effect of increased marketing has benefited the community, region and state.

First Fridays after Five, Chocolate Festival, Literary Festival, and Holiday Open House are events designed to re-acquaint locals and visitors with downtown. Print ads, a full-color brochure, website, and Facebook page are used to keep people informed and interested in Lewisburg.

The dedication, hard work, and vision of all businesses, non-profits, the community, and city government are the key to success. It is only through the group effort that we can achieve all that we do and the reason we chose the LDBA as Lewisburg's Best Idea.

★ Lexington, Kentucky

Visitors and residents alike appreciate the elegance and energy vibrating through-out Lexington. From the peaceful rolling hills of the outer protected green spaces to the excitement of the downtown, one is struck with the activity of a city constantly on the move. Art is incorporated through many means, from creatively-painted street drains, to artistically engraved garbage cans, to pulsating racing horse statues, to an eight story high mural of Abraham Lincoln, to well-maintained stately antebellum homes.

Best Idea: Town Branch Commons is currently in development. The plan calls for creating a long, linear park with a network of pools, fountains, rain gardens and pocket parks stretching from the Isaac Murphy Memorial Art Garden to Cox Street. The mayor has asked for $10M in his 2016 budget as initial infrastructure funding for this initiative. We intend to pursue additional federal and state funding for infrastructure and the Blue Grass Community Foundation has begun planning for a private capital campaign.

★ Madisonville, Kentucky

Special Mention: Heritage Preservation

Preservation has taken a strong foothold with the implementation of a Historic District Commission and the resulting designation of a large portion of the business district as an historic district. Two excellent examples of reuse include the historically significant Rosenwald School which is now a community center and the Hopkins County Library which now houses the Historical Society of Hopkins County Historical Museum.

Best Idea: The Trover Wellness Park on the Baptist Health campus is a 10-acre tract donated to the city. The park's entire development cost was funded by generous local benefactors. Many people have described the park as a peaceful sanctuary in town that lets them feel as though they are out of town. It gives people space for their minds and souls to rest and relax. The park is a Certified Wildlife Habitat.

★ Marietta, Ohio

Special Mention: Landscaped Areas

Marietta is a city of engaged residents who selflessly volunteer their time and resources to create attractive landscapes in parks, conservation areas and at businesses. They enlist all of their skills to assess, design, secure materials and skilled personnel, and install gardens, all with volunteer assistance. The results are truly remarkable.

Best Idea: The City of Marietta was awarded approximately $21,000 from the Ohio Department of Transportation to beautify the three gateways into our charming town. Marietta in Bloom members developed and executed detailed plans for the three gateways which are quickly recognized by the red brick wall with 'Marietta Founded 1788' on each. The result is show-stopping, welcoming entrances into the city for residents and guests.

★ McCall, Idaho

Special Mention: Urban Forestry

McCall's tree committee has worked to strengthen the urban forest, city trees and provide leadership to preserve, protect and expand the tree canopy. Tree ordinances were passed in 2001 and strengthened in 2008. All new development requires review by the city's certified arborist and the tree committee. The dedication of the tree committee, city staff and residents helps preserve the majestic ponderosa pines and Douglas firs throughout the community.

Best Idea: A partnership with Idaho Transportation Department and the City of McCall on replacing the Lardo Bridge was an impressive joint venture. Given the importance of the bridge to the community, city leaders and staff worked in advance of design to make sure the voice of the community was heard. Incorporating this input resulted in a bridge that has a viewing area and City Parks staff is working to gain permission to install flower baskets. The bridge provides a safe transportation route for pedestrians and bicyclists and is truly an enhancement to the city.

★ Morro Bay, California

Special Mention: Community Involvement

Morro Bay in Bloom has achieved record community involvement. They meet each week for 2 hours on Saturday morning to complete a specific task identified and planned in advance. Their tag line is: "Beautifying Morro Bay 2 Hours at a Time". Morro Bay in Bloom partners with numerous other local community and civic organizations to accomplish goals. Weekly email communications are sent inspiring residents to participate no matter their age or ability.

Best Idea: These are just three of our many ideas, any one of which could qualify as a "Best Idea".

Bike/Pedestrian Bridge: we created a safe transportation route connecting northern and southern Morro Bay for bicyclists and pedestrians of all physical abilities.

Hidden History Project: this will bring elements of Morro Bay's history into locations where the public gathers and has the potential of becoming a creative place-making project in its own right.

Rainwater Harvesting System Demonstration: The installation of an operational rainwater harvesting, storage, and dispensing system in an area that receives a lot of foot traffic shows the public a simple and effective system that will make more home and business installations possible.

★ Newtown Square, Pennsylvania

Special Mention: Heritage Preservation

Heritage preservation is a strong commitment among Newtown Square residents and businesses. Its museums, historic sites and covered bridge are lovingly cared for by dedicated individuals. Youth-related events at the various sites around town expose children to Newtown Square's unique past on a continuing basis. The long-standing Passport to History program at the Paper Mill has touched more than 100,000 students during its existence.

Best Idea: The Garrett Williamson School in Newtown Square has a unique mission to bring educational resources to needy children ages 5 through 15 in the community. For the last three years there has been an annual Plant-A-Thon in the spring whose motto is "Plant trees, sow seeds, make friends". In 2015, a remarkable addition was made to the summer camp program at the school with the construction and planting of a significant functional garden. Fenced to protect the plantings from animals, the garden is both beautiful and fruitful. It is cleverly designed to incorporate as many different learning opportunities for as many different age groups as possible. Within the garden various specialty gardens exist, including a "pizza garden," as well as areas that demonstrate companion planting of vegetables. Young people are actively engaged in sowing seeds, planting fruit trees, watering the crops and harvesting the food. This space is truly a model for an exceptional learning garden.

★ Ottawa, Illinois

Heritage sites are plentiful in Ottawa, starting with the historic downtown and a residential neighborhood on the National Register. The site of the second Lincoln-Douglas debate in 1858 has been turned into an attractive park and the debate is memorialized with larger than life sculptures of Lincoln and Douglas. Murals depicting events in the city's history can be found throughout the downtown.

Best Idea: Beginning with the massive flooding in 2008 which caused the permanent closure of the Central School on the bank of the Illinois River, the City of Ottawa has made an intensive and very successful effort to seriously upgrade its flood management practices and expertise. As a result of implementing a host of vital flood management practices, many Ottawa residents whose homes and property are located in flood zones now enjoy greatly reduced rates when paying for federal flood insurance. Another considerable advantage is the savings in tax dollars due to having fewer flood damaged properties to repair. In fact, the City of Ottawa's efforts have been so successful that Ottawa's flood management expertise is now routinely recognized on a state and even national basis. Through partnership with its Illinois State Senator, Ottawa is sharing its expertise with a coalition of cities and villages all along the Illinois River.

★ Rockford, Illinois

Special Mention: Urban Forestry

Rockford proudly wears the nickname "The Forest City". Through a wide collaboration and alliance of agencies, Rockford's urban forest has prospered. Thousands of trees have been planted to protect and improve air quality and manage water runoff. Inventories of trees along streets and in parks are maintained and are resources for managing the urban forest.

Best Idea: Community gateways are used to reflect pride and a sense of place; they are important components of the road improvement projects underway on key and historic streets in Rockford's core. Corridor projects have replaced some of the oldest utility and transportation infrastructure in the city with comprehensive planned routes with linear parks, intermodal transportation accommodations, energy efficient street lighting and landscaped boulevards/shoulders.

★ Santa Paula, California

Special Mention: Heritage Preservation

Santa Paula has a multi-faceted heritage program including four museums that honor the past – agriculture, oil discovery, aviation, and local art. Many older churches are beautifully restored, while numerous murals and monuments are placed throughout downtown, including the only monument in the United States honoring the importance of farm workers.

Best Idea: Santa Paula is committed to offer youth recreation areas that are well groomed and safe. Each weekend finds our parks filled with families attending sporting events or having family celebrations. Using Community Development Block Grants and Development Impact Fees, a million dollars went into improvements for Las Piedras Park. A new soccer field, irrigation system, athletic field lighting, basketball courts and landscaping renovated that area. America in Bloom Santa Paula agreed to put final touches on the police substation building in the park as well.

★ Saratoga, California

Special Mention: Overall Impression

Saratoga is a very clean and tidy community on the edge of Silicon Valley in California. All sectors take great pride in maintaining their properties to a high standard. Public parks are immaculately maintained and some neighborhoods have even voted to assess an additional tax to pay for landscape improvements.

Best Idea: Ten years ago, a handful of residents set their minds to beautifying downtown Saratoga, known as the Village. Today, this group is 50 strong and on any Tuesday morning or most any morning of the week, you will see the Village Gardeners at work, maintaining over 75 tree wells and 100 pots, Blaney Plaza, Turkey Trot and more; no small feat since Saratoga's mild climate dictates year round attention and the drought demands constant vigilance.

The Village Gardeners have thrived because of collaboration with local businesses and the city government which now all play a significant role. The Saratoga Village Development Council,(SVDC) a consortium of local businesses, has embraced the work of the Village Gardeners, and each compete for the coveted Golden Broom Award, a distinguished honor, bestowed on the proprietor who best maintains their store front.

The SVDC enlists the support of the Village Gardeners to ensure the Village is in shape for its monthly events which attract families and children from all over the Silicon Valley. Love Notes, the Heritage Festival, Bollywood, Tree Lighting, St. Paddy's Day are just some of the many events. The Village Gardener and SVDC list servers keep everyone informed and that information also appears on the village website, www.saratogavillage.info, the Village Gardeners Facebook page, and the Chamber of Commerce website. The City of Saratoga website provides links to all of these resources.

★ St. Charles, Illinois

Special Mention: Landscaped Areas

St. Charles has many beautifully designed and well-maintained landscapes that are varied, interesting, and colorful. Floral displays are accentuated by combinations of flowering shrubs, ornamental grasses, and evergreen foliage. The park system takes great pride in their commitment to quality landscapes throughout the city.

Best Idea: St. Charles launched a new branding initiative for its downtown embodied by the tagline "Discover Your City Side", which represents the many ways residents and visitors can enjoy urban experiences in St. Charles. Whether energized by cultural, social or culinary experiences, downtown is the heartbeat of the city, infusing vibrancy into social spaces, so people can come alive and come together with ease.

Plans are in place to incorporate our new brand into all aspects of our downtown marketing and advertising, including our downtown events. "Discover Your City Side" and the collaboration it engendered created an umbrella under which our diverse community groups could be in harmony with a common spirit, a common identity, a common brand and emulates the teamwork of those who have come together to enter St. Charles into the AIB National Awards Program.

★ Tarboro, North Carolina

Special Mention: Heritage Preservation

Tarboro, founded in 1760, is one of the oldest incorporated towns in North Carolina. The 45-block historic residential district is listed on the National Register of Historic Places. The Town Common covers 15 acres with many stately landmark trees and is one of only two historic Town Commons remaining in America. The Tarboro Historic District Commission ensures that the beauty and integrity of the heritage of Tarboro remains for all time.

Best Idea: Improvements to the urban forest are a Best Idea for Tarboro. The Main Street tree project and the long-term plans for the Town Common trees will have a lasting impact, contribute to the health of our environment, and enhance the overall appeal of our community.

The Main Street tree project evolved after years of discussion with residents, town staff and consultations with tree experts. Chinese Pistaches, European Hornbeams and Foster's Hollies were selected to provide the updated look for Main Street. An additional benefit from this project is that the smaller trees do not camouflage building facades and their architectural details.

A proposal was approved by the Tarboro Town Council for a public/private partnership to restore the historic Town Common trees involving the Rotary Club of Tarboro and the Town of Tarboro. North Carolina State University Extension specialists and the North Carolina Forestry Service have provided expertise in developing this long-term plan, which includes planting historically accurate trees as well as the proper maintenance of existing trees.

Both the projects have evolved through community involvement. Residents, town employees, civic groups and tree experts have worked together to plan and implement improvements that make a positive impact. As a result, Tarboro will have an urban forest that will benefit current residents as well as future generations.

★ Venice, Florida

Special Mention: Floral Displays

Venice provides a wonderful and dynamic example of excellence in its floral displays. Beds, baskets and container plantings were everywhere. Every display is well designed, harmonious and beautifully integrated into the cityscape. All of the floral displays were well tended and watered by a dedicated volunteer watering brigade. Drip irrigation using reclaimed water kept the flower beds in top condition.

Best Idea: The City of Venice owns and operates the Eastside Water Reclamation Facility (EWRF), a 6 million gallon (MG) per day advanced wastewater treatment plant with high level disinfection for providing reclaimed water to the city's public access reuse distribution system. The EWRF provides reclaimed water to golf courses, commercial users and residences, mainly for irrigation. The facility has one 3 MG and one 7.5 MG ground storage tank.

The city also has an 11-acre, 37 MG lined pond for storing reclaimed water. The EWRF is operated so that all reclaimed water is sent to the ground storage tanks, where it is pumped to the reuse distribution system. The reclaimed water storage pond is used as a seasonal storage pond providing storage capacity during low reclaimed water demand periods and allowing for augmentation of treated effluent from the EWRF during high reclaimed water demand periods. This allows the operations staff to limit the amount of reclaimed water discharged to surface water and maximize the amount available for distribution.

Water quality of the storage pond is poor because the water is subject to sunlight and other environmental factors, so the water is treated a second time to ensure adequate water quality is achieved. The city is upgrading this system to increase the capacity per day from 8 to 10 MG.

★ Warrenville, Illinois

Special Mention: Environmental Efforts

Warrenville has received Sierra Club's Cool Cities Award and the Environmental Advisory Committee (EAC) developed a Climate Action Plan to reduce greenhouse emissions. Warrenville's residents recycle more than 51% of their waste. Bio-swales and detention ponds with native plants throughout the city reduce storm water runoff and create habitat for wildlife. More than 60 miles of trails connect to the DuPage County Trail system, encouraging people to get out into acres of forests and natural areas.

Best Idea: When we learned the Illinois Department of Transportation (IDOT) was planning to expand State Highway Route 56 through the middle of town from two to four lanes, the city embraced the project and worked relentlessly with IDOT for more than a decade to develop and implement a design that met IDOT's requirements and was sensitive to our unique character and local expectations. Many of the city's recommended upgrades were implemented, including a new 10-foot-wide multi-use trail, countdown pedestrian signals, pedestrian areas of refuge in the new center median, black painted traffic signals/streetlights/guard rails, split-rail wood fencing, decorative sound attenuation walls, and an extensive native-material-based landscape plan.

A Streetscape Workgroup was formed to identify areas for possible enhancements to the original project. It included representatives from the city council, city staff, a consulting civil engineering firm, a consulting landscape architecture firm, the Bicycle and Pedestrian Advisory Commission, the EAC, and WIB. As a result of the workgroup's efforts, the city developed and is in the process of securing IDOT approval of preliminary engineering/design plans for a separate city streetscape enhancement project that would involve the installation of decorative streetlights in several areas, new stone city identification signs, a comprehensive wayfinding sign package, landscape enhancements, and an in-ground irrigation system.

★ Washington, Missouri

Special Mention: Urban Forestry

Ten years as a Tree City USA, Washington has received growth awards in the past couple of years. 1st and 3rd Parkways are great examples of shady, walkable canopied streets, while the Miller-Post Nature Preserve is a secluded respite with awesome large trees – the making of an interpretive center. The Maintenance Operations Standards and Arboricultural and Horticultural Specifications Manual, along with the Tree, Landscaping and Vegetation Ordinances provide direction for high quality maintenance.

Best Idea: The 175th anniversary celebration of Washington's founding has been without a doubt an extravaganza. For over two years, scores of local business people and community-minded individuals planned the details of multiple events to appeal to and involve all the residents of Washington. This was accomplished by people of all ages and from every walk of life. Community pride was never more evident in the faces and in the spirit shown during this once-in-a-lifetime celebration.

The Washington Historical Society compiled a book for purchase chronicling the story of Washington, a black tie gala was held with the current Mayor Sandy Lucy and four former mayors in attendance, a parade featuring bands, walkers in period costumes, floats, and the Budweiser Clydesdales entertained thousands of enthusiastic people lining the city's streets, windows and rooftops! The parade route ended at Lions Lake and fairground, the site of an old-fashioned picnic. Other activities included the dedication of the grave of Lucinda Owens, wife of William Owens, Washington's founder, founder's day tours, a car show and fireworks.

★ West Columbia, Texas

Special Mention: Heritage Preservation

West Columbia was the first capitol of the Republic of Texas in 1836. The Varner-Hogg Plantation State Historic Site dates back to 1824. The historic Old Columbia Cemetery is the resting place of many of Austin's "Old 300" colonists and a number of heroes of the Texas Revolution. The restored Rosenwald School serves as a tribute to the initiative of Julius Rosenwald and Booker T. Washington to educate black children in rural communities across the South after the Civil War and Reconstruction.

Best Idea: This is our first time to enter the America in Bloom national awards program. It is our Best Idea! We decided to create a demonstration project in our little downtown area by utilizing the West Columbia Economic Development Corp. Landscape Grant for businesses to purchase window boxes and planters. We will encourage volunteers to adopt-a-spot to maintain the plants.

★ Winter Park, Florida

Special Mention: Heritage Preservation

Winter Park has a wealth of historic and cultural resources within the city limits. The built environment still has a good stock of historic buildings, some of which will become a museum and/ or a place to hold various meetings. The Hannibal Square Heritage Center is one of the most noteworthy heritage efforts in Winter Park related to its African American community. Here, Winter Park residents are celebrating and showcasing their artistic and cultural uniqueness.

Best Idea: Winter Park added a Sustainability Coordinator position to the city staff in 2015. This position began purely as an effort to pick up litter in waterways but has evolved into coordinatnion of a variety of major city sustainability initiatives. This includes coordination with groups that wish to accomplish a philanthropic project in the city, student project groups and city staff members. Our Sustainability Coordinator uses social media and the city's communication department to get the word and troops out.

Our newest and most innovative signature Winter Park Event is a large marine debris abatement volunteer event (about 100 volunteers) that we host quarterly. "Watershed Cleanup" events are focused on lakes in Winter Park and provide an avenue for litter pick up and an educational opportunity for residents and visitors to learn that litter dropped on any of our streets will directly affect our precious waterways. The lakes are cleaned by scuba volunteers, while the shorelines are skimmed by boaters, rowers, canoeists, stand up paddle boarders, and kayakers. All streets within the watershed are assigned to groups and picked up simultaneously, with predetermined drop off locations for the litter bags. To date we have collected over a half ton of debris.

The Volunteer Coordinator has developed an amazing list of available volunteers and in coordination with Mead Botanical Gardens several smaller community service projects were completed this year.

★ Woodhaven, Michigan

Special Mention: Overall Impression

Woodhaven takes pride in keeping lawns mowed, streets swept and residential and public parks maintained. The Downtown Development Authority works with businesses to have them meet aesthetic standards that include addition of brick facades to all older buildings renovated in the commercial district, upgrades of parking lot landscapes, new streetlights with banners, undergrounding power lines and repairing damaged streets and sidewalks.

Best Idea: The raised garden beds at the Bares Elementary School are designed for different ages/heights of students. The beds give all children the chance to reach and care for vegetables and flowers in the raised beds.

★ 2015 Judges

We appreciate the expertise and generous donation of time by our judges, who are all volunteers.

Jack Clasen*

Evelyn Alemanni

Sue Amatangelo**

Billy Butterfield

Linda Cromer

Tony Ferrara

Bill Hahn

Ed Hooker III

Ruth Miller**

Lisa Netherland

Marlborough Packard

Kristin Pategas

Stephen Pategas

Leslie Pittenger

Alex Pearl

Bruce Riggs

Melanie Riggs

Karin Rindal

Susie Stratton

Jim Sutton**

Barbara Vincentsen

Katy Moss Warner

Diana K. Weiner

Meg Whitmer

* Chair, National Awards Program Committee

** = alternate for 2015

Ottawa, IL

This annual edition is
dedicated to our America in Bloom
family, working together to make
America a better place to live,
one community at a time.

Fairhope, AL

Giving to America in Bloom

Sponsorship opportunities are available at several levels. Donations are tax deductible to the extent allowed by law. To make a gift or become a corporate sponsor, please contact us at aib@AmericaInBloom.com. 614-453-0744.

Join the Excitement - Register for 2016

Getting your community involved with America in Bloom is a great way to generate excitement and visible improvements. Start by attending our symposium in the fall (dates and location change each year) or simply sign up for the next program. Check for symposium and registration details, and sign up for our free e-newsletter at www.AmericaInBloom.org. **Each year, the registration deadline is February 28.**

Need More Books?

Please contact the AIB office to order the Best Ideas book and more copies of this addendum or order online.

aib@AmericaInBloom.org   614-453-0744

www.AmericaInBloom.org

Thanks to Our Sponsor

Our gratitude to Mountaineer Mechanical Co. for sponsoring the printing of this addendum.

www.mountaineermechanical.com
800-905-4172